A VIEW FROM THE VALLEY

Perspectives of Aspects of: Social Phenomena in Barbados,
Caribbean Sports, and Global Issues

Philip O Hunte Dip.M.ACIM.MA

Highly Recommended

Barbados

A VIEW FROM THE VALLEY

Perspectives of Aspects of: Social Phenomena in Barbados, Caribbean Sports, and Global Issues

Highly Recommended books may be ordered through Amazon.com and other booksellers.

Hunte, Philip
A View From The Valley

ISBN: 978-1494334611

Printed in the United States of America

Dedicated to my grandmother, Mrs Adelaide Haynes, Angela, my wife, Kari and Kristin, my daughters, and Hugo Inniss, my cousin who inspired me to publish these articles.

So he who had received five talents came and brought five other talents, saying, 'Lord, you delivered to me five talents; look, I have gained five more talents besides them.' His lord said to him, 'Well done, good and faithful servant; you were faithful over a few things, I will make you ruler over many things. Enter into the joy of your lord.'

Jesus the Messiah,

(Matthew 25:20-21)

Contents

Preface

Why I Wrote This Book

I wrote the articles included in this book as a gift to the people of Barbados. They were published in the Nation Newspaper, Barbados' leading national newspaper, over approximately 2 decades.

The articles address diverse topics, and the reason for their publication is to provide another point of view for discussion.

Part 1 - Family and Youth

Ten Main Reasons for Barbados' Grave Problems

There are basically ten main reasons why there are so many problems with the youth of this country. Someone could elucidate us if these points are not valid:

1. The unstable family structure in which there is one parent, usually the mother who performs all roles;

2. The lack of a back-up to the family. The extended family structure is declining. The grandmother's and older adults who helped to discipline the young have been sidelined in geriatric hospitals and elsewhere;

3. The preoccupation of many parents with making money. Child neglect. Many parents are more concerned with supplying the material needs of their children, and not the spiritual, emotional and psychological needs of them;

4. The fact that many of the youth do not belong to an organized religion that is Christian, Moslem, Baha'i. God is no longer the center of the lives of most youth;

5. The influence of the sub-culture and the counter-culture, and their appeal to the youth of the lower classes. To many such youth, it offers some solace to the "harsh world";

6. An educational system which promises a lot; but in many cases fails to allow the youth to attain their full potential;

7. Cultural penetration. The violence, sex and drugs on the TV screen. The portrayal of foreign values and culture, the easy life.

   The get rich quick syndrome where success is measured in terms of pretty cars, houses, fame, money and power, and the de-emphasising the fact that these material things are usually attained through toil, effort and sacrifice.

8. The lack of good role models. Most of the heroes of the young are the basketball heroes, foreign footballers and dub artists; and not our cricketers, academics and hard workers who have attained success through discipline and industry;

9. The fact that in Barbados the individual is known by what he owns, who he knows, who he associates with, and the social or other group to which he belongs. Many youth are aware of this and the easy way around it is to cop out; and

10. The fact that in this society, many youth are not given an ear. This is important because the young are the leaders of tomorrow and their talents should be scouted and exposed as early as possible.

Parents Must Take Control of Their Children

We should stop blaming children for their behavior. Children manifest what they are taught by their parents and from their peers.

Adults display several bad traits to their children and then when children repeat this behavior we blame them.

Free the children from the blame. There is no spiritual teaching in many households. No moral examples to follow and children tend to display what they see at home.

At sports events and other gatherings some of the lewdest behavior is exhibited. They do the "dog". They no longer cheer at sports.

Many gyrate and behave in ways which are worse than their charges. Many do not attend Parent-Teacher Association meetings, neither are they interested in the progress of their children. Brand–name gear and material things are their only interest.

Many are unwilling to invest in their children's future, yet fork out thousands in legal fees when their children break the law.

Parents, face to your responsibilities; you are the stewards of your children.

Parents Must Know Their Roles in Today's World

In these times it is an onerous and tiring exercise to raise children, with the influences and pressures placed on them.

The problems which face children today would make those of two or three decades ago seem like child's play. Most kids today are materially better off and they have access to more amenities, educational and social, than their parents.

Parents must be aware of their roles. The main functions of a parent are to clothe, feed, provide shelter, educate and train children.

Discipline and chastisement are essential to the rearing of balanced individuals. There is no cut-off age, but it is an accomplishment when a parent can rear a child through adolescence and a rapport between the two still exists.

Those who fail to perform their duties abdicate and forfeit their roles as parents. No amount of material things can substitute for instilling values and virtues in their children. Today, children may still need financial support in their 20s, especially if they are doing tertiary studies.

The situation calls for a dual role by parents. The mother is the first educator, but the role of the father is equally important. A father who fails to educate his children forfeits his rights to fatherhood.

The only obligations of children are obedience and respect for their parents - and by extension God. The reason for having children is not to anticipate support in our old age; although some attempt to show gratitude to their parents in this manner.

More Jails Won't Solve the Problem

The time is ripe to take serious remedial action to help the youth of Barbados or else there will be dire consequences as the 21st century ushers in.

Many of our youth come from social situations in which they were not loved and cherished, not even by their parents. Proper values were not inculcated in them. They never experienced the sense of belonging to immediate relatives, society, or the nation.

More jails will not solve the problem. The regular clang of the gallows at Dodds will not solve the problem, as some tend to believe and are clamouring for. The death penalty for the more heinous and barbaric crimes could be used as well as community service.

The problem with the youth needs to be tackled at the source. Values such as the family, parental responsibility, education, respect for oneself and others, respect for the property of others, the need to be disciplined, the way to speak and dress, genuine etiquette and how to spend money wisely or otherwise. The work ethic needs to be taught in schools, so that the young can appreciate the value of hard work and its rewards.

Spiritual qualities need to be taught. There is nothing mystical about these.

They are not based on emotional and noisy escapades, where frustrations can be vented, neither, are they clothed in dogma and ritualistic or philosophical postulations, but such qualities as truthfulness, trustworthiness, the realization of the Almighty God, acceptance and experiencing Him, loving Him and seeking to acquire virtues like sensitivity, sharing, caring for our families and fellow men our spouses and children.

Being of service to our fellow man and adhering to the concept of the brother-hood of man and the human family. Any program which does not emphasise the foregoing is short-changing our youth.

Only We Can Help Our Youth

It is with awe that we view that increasing incidence of violence in Barbados.

Violence has trickled into every aspect of our lives, including the schools, where pupils of one of the more reputable schools have been arrested for causing a fracas.

Further investigation has revealed that many youth leave home armed with sophisticated weapons, which have no place in a classroom and which can be used only to maim and disfigure.

Many of our youth seem to be in a state of paranoia; where they believe that others are out to get them. This feeling can only be got rid of by counseling and by genuine interest and love of the older generation.

But, many adults seem to be stricken by a paralysis of ideas toward helping the youth. There seems to be a lost generation in Barbados.

The majority of the youth in this country have conditions at their disposal which hardly existed two generations ago. The facilities at schools are largely better. There are more flexible curricula and the choice of vocations is greater, yet may young people fail to realize that their potential is limitless.

There are even guidance counselors to advise on study methods, and how to handle conflicts and plan careers.

A lot of the blame would seem to lie in the families from which these youth originate. Where are the parents? Peer pressure would seem to be another cause of the increasing violence. How can a child leave under its parent's roof armed with knives and other weapons.

As a public gesture, some sort of sociological study should be carried out to ascertain the cause of this increasing violence. It should not be an academic exercise as such, but ideas as to resolution of the problem should be solicited.

Many parents seem willing to sacrifice limb, life and soul to see their children through life; not remembering that discipline, imparting of values, character building, respect for others and their property and honesty and trustworthiness are of paramount importance.

Children should be exposed to hardships, or sometime in the future this society will degenerate into a nation of sissies and brats. Provision of material sustenance is not all. We yearn for the old grandmothers, strong leaders, both secular and religious.

The declining influence of the family and the lack of positive role models are two reasons why the youth are disillusioned. Their homes have failed many of them. The school is failing them and there is a lack of respect for church leaders and the powers of politicians has waned very sharply.

The problem needs to be solved here in Barbados and not by solutions imported from other countries, where they have failed and are sure to fail here.

Young People Are Trapped in Lost Values

It seems it is going to take an act of divine intervention to free the youth of Barbados from the morass in which many of them have found themselves.

This generation should be the one which is more enlightened than previous ones; after all, more money has been invested in educational facilities and in many instances, social amenities and economic conditions are vastly superior to many years ago.

There seems to be no end to the delinquent youth who daily flout the law and threaten the long-established traditions and institutions which have been the bastion of Barbadian society for decades, and of which, although in some need to reform, Barbadians are proud and even boast of it to foreigners.

Today there seems to be a very strong anti-police sentiment by many of the youth.

The society seems to be throwing up a generation of clones in which there is hardly any individual thought, and in which (the gun violence, the butcher's knife and the cutlass) seems to be the only means of resolving conflict and even differences of opinion. Drugs are being used even on the streets. Women, especially the young have been targeted.

There are hardly any personal goals or tangible achievements to which many youth aspire. Parenting of balanced young people is an ever more difficult exercise. Who to blame?

The problem with the youth does not seem to be sectional but cuts across classes. The situation of the full scale aping of North American values is even more devastating to this society.

Whereas many hippies and junkies were rehabilitated, our social quitters are likely to end up at Dodds or the Psychiatric Hospital. Barbados simply does not have the resources to adopt those false values.

The writing on our youth, the publicity given to their exploits and actions are now voluminous.

No one institution in the country can solve the problem. Neither the church, the police, the punitive and remedial institutions can solve it alone. It is going to take a national effort and prayer to save the society and rehabilitate this lost generation.

Barbados simply does not have the resources to turn around these false values. It is going to take a national effort and prayer to pull back the society and rehabilitate these lost generations.

Marketing to Tweens

The tween segment of the market i.e. the pre-adolescent to 14 years comprises a significant portion of consumers. Some marketers describe it as the 'richest generation in history. There is a vast array of disposable goods and leisure products designed especially for this segment, which consists of sophisticated consumers and is any marketer's dream.

This dream can become a nightmare with the average tween consuming endless hours of commercials in any given year. The time spent by many children using social media without any figures may far exceed that spent at school. Their spending power continues to increase like their leisure time.

At six months of age a normal baby can imitate sounds like 'ma ma' and James Mc Neal the author of "Kids and Customers," brand loyalty can be influenced from about age two when kids are forming these mental images. Children according to him can recognize brand logos. Experts say that individual lifetime consumers may be worth tens of thousands of dollars.

That the constant advertising by television and radio stations enables today's tweens to surf the net with several windows open simultaneously, while having the television running, an i-pad on and friend on the phone line. This is relaxation period.

Early exposure to these media generates long term loyalty i.e. the cradle to the grave 'marketing strategy' although an unfavourable brand experience might affect their later brand choices. Tweens follow their groups when making choices, rather than individual commitments, although key members of the group need to be made comfortable. Tweens are not committed, because they would be less flexible to change. If they prove slow to adopt a brand they may be isolated and left alone.

With product life cycles shortened to months and even days with some products, rather than years, the wish list of tweens has increased, and personal identity has shifted from the 'mind' to the 'physical'. Tweens are what they eat, use wear and what they play. Branding of products has created an identity in them of what they represent rather than what they are. The trend from the adults continues. It is not uncommon to see parents purchasing Nike, La Gear, Tommy Hilfiger and other popular brands and the dependency will be driven by the kids themselves and their parents.

The cradle to the grave myth that marketers have believed for years can now be dispelled for brands that exclude tweens are likely to face many challenges when they get older. Brands are careful to make a mark on young minds that will be etched in their 'psyche' when they get older. Tweens' loyalty bears little relationship to what they may patronize when they're older.

Brands place consumers in the centre of their advertisements Coca Cola 'Life tastes good'. Xbox 'Life is short, play more'. Nintendo 'Life's a game'. The slogans influence and frame our attitudes usually outlining a pathway to a better and more fulfilled life. The advertisements portray personal happiness, beauty, comfort, from using a specific brand, but tweens need to be offered the opportunity to opt out. Successful brands offer the opportunity to choose and change the result is that they need to have several brands at their disposal

Fewer kids play on the streets. The majority are into the digital age, electronic screens (iPods and iPads), mobile phones, personal computers and more so the internet. Opportunities for merchandising have taken centre stage. Brands encompass online and offline worlds. The different linkages that brands straddle prolongs the life cycle of their product portfolios.

Entertainment products owe their survival to the motivators. For tweens perception is more important that reality. In essence this is the spirit of branding.

Parenting

Parents are the stewards of their children until such time as they can fend for themselves. They are roles which have to be played as parents and these are basically, physical, emotional and spiritual. They range from providing food, clothing and shelter the basic survival needs to spiritual moral education and formal education. Essentially we are to provide a nurturing, safe, secure, stimulating and encouraging environment within which our children can flourish.

Not to provide these would be reneging on our duties, hence the need to acquire parenting skills. Women are the first educators of children and it is necessary that they be educated foremost and that they have control over their fertility and be able to rear their children without the deprivation and constraints of past generations. But they will only rise from being the last class in most societies, through education, in its broadest sense and legislation to back their rights.

Children on the other hand are obligated to respect their parents, show homage, look after their parents, especially when they are old, offer prayers for their parents, who are their life givers. By respecting and obeying their parents by extension they are obeying God. In modern times the role of the parents should be equal though not the same.

In an age of enlightenment and material advancement, we must be cautious not to substitute good parenting with material gadgets. We must contribute to the socialisation of our progeny. Young children are like sponges soaking up almost everything in their external environment. The sooner we expose them to the positive influence the better. There are many negative forces which capture the young especially 'the counter culture' which is highlighted on our airwaves, the visual media, literature and these are having a devastating effect on the young, the tip of the iceberg which we are now seeing.

Young people today are more daring and adventurous as a result of the technological revolution, as manifest in the Internet, television, travel and through the availability of learning material Moreover, they are being exposed to these media at earlier and earlier stages of their lives. As parents we have to regulate the dosage, time and the type of media to which we expose our children. Knowledge is doubling every 2 years and things which the baby boomers learnt in their tweens are now available to today's children as early as primary school. We must be selective to what we expose our young people.

We should also be aware of the friends of our children as well as their parents. The social groups to which they belong and the opinion leaders and their characters. We should encourage wholesome pastimes, give them a voice in decision making as they mature, easing the reigns of control on them as they gain experience, but always remembering that a family is a hierarchy.

So as parents we should in no way hinder or retard the progress of our children. In this global village, as always, we need to see the nobility of our children. They are "our most valuable resource and our most vulnerable charge". They need and crave love, discipline, direction and protection. They need spiritual, intellectual and physical tools not merely to survive in the 'rat race' and ' jungle' which pervades this civilization, but in order to navigate the pitfalls of youth in the greater society, and be rare beacons, shining examples of nobility, so rare in this world.

Education

Education should be a drawing out or a development of a student's potential to the fullest extent possible. Contemporary education is concerned only with a presentation of information, rather than a drawing out of potential. Schools are primarily a place where facts and ideas are dispensed by teachers and stored by pupils. As a consequence diplomas and degrees do no more than certify that certain amounts of information were dispensed and that the recipients of these certifications were able to demonstrate at various points during the course of their formal education that they had stored the information long enough for it to be retrieved and written down in an examination.

Degrees and diplomas say very little about the character of their recipients, character meaning their ability to apply this knowledge constructively and express love to humanity. A school system based on the narrow concept of dispensing information can and will never adequately serve the needs of society.

True education should train humanity for their highest station - servitude. Education must be concerned with the whole person, his self-esteem and self-actualization, rather than a part of him.

Every school should cater to the needs of its students in drawing out their potential, polishing their character and dignity and spiritual qualities and not only seeking to place them in societal slots.

In concluding, no teacher should give up hope on their pupils. They have the ability to help in polishing these rough diamonds into making a mark on these tabula rasas.

Part 2 - Sports

Get Legends to Work With West Indies Team

Caribbean cricket enthusiasts and advocates are yearning for the day when those who represent us give us more consistently good performances.

They should not subject us to angina or other cardiac ailments, especially when, with a little more application and discipline, they can avoid snatching defeat from the jaws of victory, an act at which they have become seemingly adept in recent times.

The current West Indies team has structural problems, one of which is being unable to bowl their opponents out twice in a match.

Essentially, this is how matches are won, although some declaration decisions may backfire on the declarants.

In addition, the main players lack a true professional approach to the game, and this is even more glaring when they have faulty techniques and limited abilities.

The opposition know how to dislodge our batsmen and how to handle our bowlers. The flaws in our cricketers' techniques are constantly being exposed and the irony is that those at fault seem unable to remedy these flaws through rigorous practice, heeding the advice of the legends, discipline and hard work.

The team continues to perform fairly well in the shorter version of the game but, unfortunately, it seems to carry the same approach into the Test matches.

One wonders sometimes if the handsome rewards which the players receive are their overriding motivation.

In the recent **Champions Trophy** when Clive Lloyd was around there was an inkling of improvement in performance but, immediately afterwards, it was back to the spasmodic regime to which we have become accustomed.

There seems to be reverence for some of the greats, so there is no reason why these greats should not have a role in the team's preparation and psychological build-up to matches.

The pride of the players of the pristine era of the West Indies cricket is sorely lacking. Caribbean cricketers need to get rid of their fear of the Brits, the Aussies, New Zealanders and Pakistanis. These cricketers are only human and can be beaten.

With team spirit and some more aggression, this team can be in the upper tier of world cricket.

Athletes Can Endorse Products

Ronald "Suki" King, Obadele Thompson and Andrea Blackett are names synonymous with success in sports. Our businesses should be using these sporting successes as brands to sell merchandise and endorse products.

Such a venture would not only sell products here and overseas but it would put money in the pockets of these three luminaries. The sight of "Suki" King having to wash cars to defend one of his world titles is most distasteful.

This venture would depend on if and where the legal concept of image rights occurs in our laws. Image rights is name, fame and image which is basically how these sportsmen should be viewed by consumers. Names have a draw back in that they are difficult to register as trademarks, which are guarantees to buy goods because they show a representation of their heroes.

Without legislation, image right could be deemed as "passing off". Sportsmen would need to prove that they own the goodwill of the attraction which brings custom. Our athletes would need to change around their image frequently, using different apparel and hairstyles in the effort to lessen the unauthorized use of their image. They would have to make photographs of themselves quickly so as to render older images obsolete and prevent unauthorized use of them.

Use of these athletes in advertising and communication strategies can enhance the sales of businesses and at the same time enhance their financial status.

End May Justify the Means

We note with some expectation that the West Indies cricket team is being coached by an Australian. It is a truism that the best sportsmen do not always make the best coaches for some reason or the other. Perhaps, our cricketers will respond to an expatriate of different ethnic and cultural stock, at least for the sake of avid and arrant Caribbean cricket supporters.

But what magic wand will Bennet King wave?

We had such cricket icons as sir Viv Richards, Clive Lloyd, Malcolm Marshall, may peace be upon his soul, and Andy Roberts; they could not make a mark on the performance of our cricketers.

Sometimes we have to go rock bottom, before we can rise to our true potential.

One would have thought that, given the fact that most of our players are of one ethnic group, from the same region, having the same legacy as the illustrious West Indians, who tried, either to coach or to manage them, who are aware of the effect of cricket on the psyche of Caribbean people, that our cricketers would have responded and brought some joy to supporters.

No, what we had to do is to import a coach from the land of our archrivals, and what we are now seeing is a new spirit, a new alacrity by some players who were perpetrating a syndrome of mediocrity.

The position of West Indies cricket, just above Zimbabwe and Bangladesh is nothing to evoke any feeling of bliss in the Caribbean players or supporters, for that matter.

Let us not be in any way flattered by our performance in the ICC Cup. It was a breath of fresh air, and perhaps a wake-up call. Caribbean cricket lovers would wish that somehow the team can improve and be on the upturn, back to the pristine era of the late '70s and the '80s.

Some detractors may lament the fact that we have had to employ an expatriate, an Australian, of different ethnic origin. Even a type of backward or retrogressive move or even neo-colonialist move but a Machiavellian tactic is how I see it.

Something had to be done to stop the downward slide which we experienced, and here, the ends hopefully will justify the means.

Long Live Windies, the Kings of Cricket

West Indians have witnessed a hilarious series of cricket in which we have again asserted our dominance. Like true kings, we came from one down and inflicted a crushing defeat on the English team.

From the outset, it could have been argued that this English team could hardly have done any worse than its predecessors which were vanquished 5-0 on two occasions and 4-0 out the other. This English team, enthusiastic, eager and to some extent underrated, performed at a higher standard than was expected of it.

In the first Test, the champions played badly. Poor batting, bowling and fielding led to our defeat. The second was washed out. The third, although more even, could and should have gone to the English had it not been for the rain.

In the fourth the great champions began to wake up. Superb batting by Haynes, Best and Richards, and magnificent bowling by Ambrose sealed the fate of the English, although their efforts were almost undone by poor fielding.

The men were now being separated from the boys. Despite the cries about poor umpiring and cheating, the champs reigned supreme.

The same umpires who were now questioned had just been deemed good, when their decisions were in favour of the tourists.

One only has to remember Gooch on 17 runs on the first day of the Test in Trinidad – that lbw decision.

The fifth Test was the climax. The two Barbadian greats, Haynes and Greenidige, gave the English a practical exercise in batsmanship. The theoretical concept of the "corridor of uncertainty", so rigidly adhered to by the English bowlers in the earlier Tests now became "the corridor of death and plunder".

Anything fractionally short was cut with sheer savagery and anything pitched up was caressed with precision through the covers, or midoff, or driven with the force of a typhoon.

The series was one of the most enjoyable we have seen in a long time. Many were shocked by the first Test defeat, but champions have bad days.

The journalists who came here, some of them knowing no more about cricket than the theory of plate tectonics, did a lot of damage, by trying to turn little incidents into issues and personal vendettas, in their effort to feed the British Press.

To the English, well done! You sure outdid yourselves! Do come again and enjoy our sun, beaches and lessons in batsmanship and bowling.

To our boys, keep up the good work! Show Pakistan later this year and the Aussies next year what is true calypso cricket.

Call for Changes in Cricket

Brian Lara's decision to forgo the trip to Australia this month has caused a lot of reaction in Barbados and the West Indies because of his Importance to the team and cricket's importance to the West Indies.

Brian Lara is today's batting supremo. He is what Vivian Richards and Sir Garfield Sobers were in their eras. No Tendulkar, Inzaman or Steve Waugh can even hope to claim to this status, despite computer or whatever other ratings or criteria are used. They are mere pretenders to his throne!

The reasons for Lara's actions are still nebulous. If it is fatigue, stress, or any grievance or problem they should have been clearly revealed and we would all sympathise with this genius. He is human though, and different individuals have different levels of tolerance to situations. West Indies cricket is at the crossroads. We have been dethroned as kings of the sport. Mark Taylor said that he would defeat us, at home, and he did.

Where are the vaunted fast bowlers? Walsh near the end of his days, although the most consistent in recent times. Ambrose a shadow of his old self, Kenny Benjamin promising but having problems with discipline. Bishop not as devastating as before. Richardson near the end of his days, and not the ideal captain. Hooper enigmatic, promising a lot but yet to deliver after nearly a decade.

West Indies cricket to me is in the stage where it was in the late 60s and early 70s. The old stagers are longish in the tooth and we are losing. Now is the time for the West Indies Cricket Board of Control to implement radical changes designed to put West Indies cricket back at the pinnacle of world cricket.

At this juncture, on present form, no present West Indian player, could hold his place in the West Indies team of the late 70s, or early 80s except king Lara!

Give Lara the captaincy and this should be motivational enough to rekindle his fire. To be a true professional one must be tough. To Lara, enjoy the glitter and wealth but stick in there.

At 26, he has a potentially long future ahead of him. The wealth and records are there for the taking, given his skills and talents. He has already been entrusted with the mantle of leadership; and now is the time for higher ground

Form a nucleus of young talented, discipline players with Lara at the helm and West Indies cricket is on the right path.

Past performances are for posterity. It is time for the old guard to go and those with potential and talent to come forward. Make Lara talent to come forward. Make Lara leader and we are on the right path!

Fast Bowlers Really Running Things Now

The stories of the West Indies cricket team, though partly due to a great team spirit, excellent batting bowling and fielding and inspirational captaincy, has be attributable more so to a spate of fine fast bowlers which our islands have been producing.

In Hall and Griffith, we thought that we had the ultimate pair of fast bowlers. Barbados was then the headquarters for these men of pace; but since the mid-1970s, we have seen the headquarters change to other territories: from Messrs. Roberts, Holding and Croft, Marshall and Garner from Barbados and Ambrose, Bishop and Walsh.

These gentlemen have done us proud through their exhibition of the art of fast bowling. They have been capable of hurling that five-ounce missile at speeds, sometimes in excess of 90 miles per hour.

To combat them, opposing batsmen need nerves of steel, good technique, good eyesight, coordination, reflexes like a cheetah and guts. Unfortunately, few batsmen have been able to withstand these gentlemen.

The authorities have imposed first, the front foot rule and now the one bouncer per over in an effort to quell the prowess of these men of pace, but to no avail.

They have the guile, the tact and the arsenal to prise out the opposition batsmen: from Yorkers to big in- and out-swingers, many of which are unplayable. There is no respite for their opponents.

Gone are days when opposing batsmen could block out the genuine fast bowler and score freely from the other bowlers. When opposing batsmen try to evade one from the striking end, another one is there to "torment" at the other end.

It is alarming the West Indies is still in a state of rebuilding, yet we are still champions. A few good middle order batsmen will prolong our reign as kings into the 21st Century.

Every victory by our cricket team gives us a high. It makes us feel important and stamps our authority over the rest of the world in this sport. We experience a feeling of importance which we do not achieve in any other sphere of activity. There is unity and harmony among all West Indians when another of our opponents bites the dust.

Give us cricket all year round that we can experience a feeling of importance and take our rightful place up there among the larger nations. Long live the sovereignty of cricket! We are the true kings!

Part 3 - Independence and Culture

Urgent Need to Conserve Water

Barbados should never be deemed a water scarce country. On average we receive annually between 60 and 70 inches of rain in the wetter parishes; St. Thomas, St. George, St Joseph, and the dryer parishes receive around 40 inches annually.

We need better conservation measures and not solely to depend on our aquifers for our portable and irrigation water. Too much water is allowed to run off the roofs of buildings and is lost.

Dams can be built for the storage of water and underground tanks as suggested for new buildings, like in Bermuda which uses this system as the main source for all their water.

Each new house should have a sizable water tank.

Water is allowed to run off many huge public buildings and end up in the sea where it is lost to future use.

When one compares Barbados with Israel we are well blessed with water resources.

In Israel there are dust storms and rainfall is very seasonal; yet there is adequate potable water, bountiful agriculture with oranges, wheat, bananas, olives and a variety of vegetables.

The luxuriance of the country is taken to its peak at the Baha'i Gardens on Mount Carmel, which at the turn of the 20th Century was a desert.

Barbadians should implement conservation measures, recycle, reuse and generally use this precious resource more sparingly. Let desalination be a last resort.

Bad Time to Foul Up

Mr. Edward Cumberbatch has again been warning us about the pollution of our water supply. The problem with our environment seems to be one of attitude. Many people no longer care about their surroundings. A look along the road sides and highways reveal all sorts of house hold garbage, food containers, old clothes and so on.

A lot of the garbage consists of plastic which does not readily decompose. Suck-wells which used to drain the fields and replenish the water supply have been choked and neglected. A film shown on a clean-up campaign is what sensitized me to the gross neglect of our environment, when dead dogs, sheep and all sorts of garbage were seen in some of our gullies.

Cattle egrets, black birds and fish have died, the result of our indiscretion. Furthermore, chemical fertilisers and pesticides have been said to find their way into the sea, where they do irreparable damage to the coral reefs and further deplete our fish population. Again destroying our marine life and having a direct effect on tourism and coastal protection.

The need to diversify agriculture and the dense population of Barbados, as well as the number of pests and crop diseases, has made it necessary for farmers to use pesticides and herbicides to increase their yield. Excessive use of chemical on plants can affect the consumers of such food. As yet, there seems to be no vigorous organization to monitor chemical residues in plants and good crops.

Our clean water supply is vital to the economy. It only takes one serious incident of pollution and our tourist product will be hampered. Barbadians can no longer boast of the cleanest water supply in the world when our experts point out that it is being polluted. Barbados does not want to become like Poland and some other eastern European countries where as little as two per cent of their estimated water reserves are potable.

We as Barbadians need to bequeath to future generations a clean environment like the one we inherited from our fore-parents. It is not hoped that a disaster will be necessary to drive us to our senses. New laws may help to curb littering and pollution, but farmers also need to be educated as to the prudent use of pesticides and weedicides before it is too late.

Sugar's Days Almost Done

The University of Newcastle's Geography Department has just spent two weeks surveying almost a quarter of the island's arable land and among other things, they have found that since 1985, 24 per cent of the land surveyed has gone out of active arable cultivation.

Also, that 8.5 per cent of this has been developed or is about to be developed and lost to agriculture; six percent mostly in St. Thomas is in pasture for dairy and beef cattle; and 9.5 per cent is laying idle.

These findings only serve to quantify what Dr. Colin Hudson has been saying: that the island has been losing its arable land at an alarming rate.

From the estimation, it is clear that if this trend continues, there will soon be hardly any arable land left in the country. To some extent, it reflects the fact that agriculture, especially sugar production as an economic activity, is declining. Housing and other forms of activity are replacing sugar; and we must ask why.

It is grossly unprofitable to produce sugar here on any scale. Many small farmers realized this years ago when they encountered a myriad of problems from having their lands ploughed, the high over heads involved in cultivating, fertilizing, reaping and even having their canes transported to the factories.

Moreover, the returns from their crops were usually less than the expenditure involved.

The price that we now pay for sugar is much more than we would pay if we had to finally curtail our sugar production and import from say Cuba, Brazil or one of the other larger, cheaper sugar producers.

The only factors which seem to prolong sugar's life span are national pride, the vested interest of a few planters, the fact that it helps reduce unemployment and it is still a foreign exchange earner.

Perhaps, if one had to look at the age structure of those involved in sugar production, the results might show the percentage of youth involved in the industry and the skills level of these workers.

This is not an effort to degrade those working in the industry, especially the art of cane cutting, but it is a back-breaking, pains-taking form of employment, which is only short-term and will not attract most Barbadians given the historical stigma attached to sugar cultivation, its tedium and the returns to the employees.

When one looks at mechanization of the sugar industry, one sees that this has been tried, and fairly successfully by some. But it is a costly exercise which is not practical in all instances.

Hand cultivated and reaped canes were the best. Some experts have stressed the drawbacks of mechanical sugar cultivation, which include soil compaction, too high ratoons, uprooting of ratoons which reduces yield in the following years' harvests, and soil damage.

There is also a woeful wastage brought about by improper loading. Tonnes of canes are lost along our road sides and burning in a persistent menace.

It is okay to say that land could easily be brought back into cultivation, but farmers are plagued by the threat of praedial larceny, high cost, the threat of crop failure and insecure markets.

The present land tenure system is such that many who would desire to go into agriculture are prevented from doing so because they do not have the means to do so.

At many of the sugar plantations, old archaic methods of management still exist. Do farmers, especially, sugar farmers put aside profits for reinvestment? Do they practice crop rotation? Are they thrifty and efficient? How long can their inefficiencies be subsidized?

The amount of sugar which we produce is negligible, in terms of world production; our market share of world sugar production could easily be met by Brazil or other cane sugar producing areas. There is also competition from other sweetening agents.

When the old sage made the comment that he would have liked to wake up one morning and not see a cane blade, that statement was sacrilege at the time, almost insane: but times have changed and sugar is no longer king.

It seems as though the fate of agriculture lies in rationalizing the whole activity, including a radical reform in land tenure, concentrating on products which are in constant demand, market gardening, meat and dairy products. The days of sugar seem to be numbered and efforts to resuscitate it seem too costly and difficult to perform. There is need for urgent remedial action if it is to survive

The Hard Road to Independence

The question of political independence is talked about in several spheres.

Political independence entails having a cultural identity, with all of the cultural artifacts, mores and norms remaining intact and being passed on for posterity.

This also entails national unity, a statement that we are Barbadians and are united.

No county is truly independent in the world today. Belonging to blocs, federations and other political and economic bodies of necessity means that part of our sovereignty has to be surrendered.

The developed countries through the IDB, World Bank and IMF, have made it compulsory that we remain dependent, especially the non-white countries. We are dependent on them for food, technology, goods and services which we ourselves can supply in some instances of even substitute.

But, even the mighty United States, the only nation on earth that has the potential to produce all it needs, the bread basket of the world, is dependent on the rest of the world for oil, food and even technology for strategic and economic reasons. It has now for the first time become a food deficit country and this does not augur well for the rest of the world, particularly Third

World countries which cannot or in some cases, would not become food efficient.

Independence is mainly hinged around having a national consciousness, identity and pride. We are moving towards this phenomenon; but after colonialism it is a giant task.

To be socialized in the traditional Bajan way, to use one's foods, have a national dress, national music, build one's houses in a distinct way, speak in a certain way, produce cultural products, and to be "craftsmen of our fate" is the task we have to make.

Making an indelible mark in the cultural and economic scheme in this world order is the task ahead of us.

Downsizing Not the Path to Follow

It would appear as though every trend that is followed in the developed countries has to be adopted in Barbados. The latest trend to be followed is downsizing.

This process, started in the United States, was an effort to meet technological changes, the changing market structure, to boost the competitiveness of transnational giants, like IBM and General Motors, who incidentally laid-off countless thousands of workers.

The slogan was to make these companies leaner and trimmer, to cut costs, and moreover increase the profitability and efficiency of these corporations in the face of increased competition.

We in Barbados do not need to take this route. Are we becoming a nation where economic considerations out-weigh every other consideration?

With a population of approximately 288, 000, the size of a modest town in big countries, we don't need to go down this road. The reality in Bim is that over 90 per cent of its denizens must work in order to have some food on their tables.

With the limitations of size and resources all efforts should be geared toward employment generation and preservation, in an effort to lessen the endemic and chronic unemployment, which is a feature of this country.

Multinational, monopolistic and oligopolistic companies which have healthy bottom lines and little or no competition in particular, can influence price, they have almost total market share and hence generate very large profits.

Downsizing is probably acceptable in the United States; where redundant workers have a chance of being reabsorbed in some other economic activity, but with little resources and limited alternatives this practice is unacceptable to most Barbadians.

We must devise means of dealing with changes in the market place and not lay off workers as a first resort. Better marketing is the answer, including retraining and re-indoctrination and a change in mindset.

After all, companies should have a social responsibility to their workers more so, to the customer who patronize them, to the environment, both physical and market place; because in the long run these are the factors which ultimately determine whether companies prosper or fold up.

Bajan Roots Withering Under Class System

Barbados has become a nation divided mainly along social lines as much as along racial lines. The reasons for this division are myriad and stand to hamper the development of the country, especially its social consciousness.

With the democratization of education there has been a trend for those who have become socially mobile to move away from the traditional areas of their birth, usually away from the rural village areas.

They have moved into the gardens, terraces and even heights, and concomitantly they have left a glaring vacuum in the villages.

Traditional village life, though, usually very rich in culture and social setting, in many cases has always lacked social amenities like playing fields, proper roads and recreational facilities in which the youth could hone their talents and creative skills. In many cases the only social outlet was the rum shop.

Today, when one visits many of these rural villages it seems as though these areas are only populated by the educational under-achievers, social misfits and losers. The old community spirit is lacking, unemployment is rife. Drugs are rampant and the youth tend to have no purpose in life.

The movement away from these areas by the more fortunate, who manage to gain social mobility through secondary and tertiary education, has left a void in these villages.

This void has been created and has allowed the underworld of crime, drug barons, gun runners and other manipulators to infiltrate.

There's hardly anyone to enlighten these village youth, there are not many proper socialization agents especially since many mothers are at work, many grandmothers have been superannuated and youth are heavily influenced by foreign lifestyles.

We have betrayed the youth because we have failed to mingle with them except on a very casual basis. The new members of the middle class fail the youth when one only sees them in their air-condition cars, windows rolled up and tinted, like the old aristocracy.

It is only necessary to go back two or three decades and we'll see that many members of this middle class came from these same villages. There was a commonality of origin – the chattel house, the oil lamp and poverty.

The new terraces and gardens are heavily populated by the same people who came from the rural villages. To some extent, these areas have some of the traits of the villages only with a higher degree of sophistication.

Where has the old plantocracy gone?

This is not a very difficult question to answer. Unless there is a gallant effort by the black middle class, the rural villages especially those on the plantations will sink into further decadence.

There needs to be a mingling of our role models with villagers. The intellectuals need to mix with the masses, despite the fact that many intellectuals are viewed with some contempt. Moreover, these role models need to be positive and give the youth targets at which to aim.

Looking at Prices and Demand

Price is an important variable in the mix of factors influencing customer demand. It is one of the most complex decisions facing the marketer.

He has to take into consideration demand, image and consumer perception when setting the price of a product. Price must be competitive and consistent with image, yet high enough to cover costs and maximize demand.

Barbadians are to a great extent, forced to pay high prices, although we are not always in agreement with the relationship between the price and quality. Marketers can draw customers' attention to price and lead to unfavourable price comparison.

There was once a retail outlet in Barbados, which had year- round "sales" and this company now had difficulties in regaining previous market share. Loss leaders are products or services sold at margins lower than normal in order to attract customers who might buy other items at normal prices.

Some supermarkets offer some products at very low, loss-making prices. Shoppers who patronize these outlets are then expected to do all their shopping at these outlets, so that profit earned from the normally priced items, more than compensate for the losses on the other items.

The loss-leader pricing is therefore a form of sales promotion and also a pricing policy, which recognizes the inter-relationship between the price and demand for one product and the price and demand for other products.

We usually cannot expect too many price cuts because the market in Barbados is small and when prices are cut, market share and profit cannot be highly enhanced.

There are relatively too few players in the market place. The discount outlets carry a range of loss-leaders and normally priced goods.

Retailers in Barbados have had the option of maintaining existing prices with the hope of losing small market share, hence for them it is more profitable to keep prices at their existing levels, especially if the outlet has an up-market image, ambience, customers with a high disposable income, wide product ranges and service.

Reducing prices would tend to increase the market share, so that in this case, the customer is the main beneficiary of price reductions. Reductions in prices should contain items which are the greatest demand, and are essential items to customers, and which have now become more and more inaccessible through the high and ever rising prices.

Hassle Free Ways to Break into Foreign Markets

Some food for thought for Barbadian manufacturers seeking to gain entry into international market. Evaluating the options, it would appear that indirect marketing is the most favourable.

Barbadian-buying offices could be established within subsidiaries of overseas businesses set up in Barbados to buy Barbadian goods. Buyers would thus buy from Barbados in the normal manner and arrange their own shipment overseas.

Export houses could also be established, encouraging foreign-owned buyers. Long established manufacturers could be encouraged to establish joint owned export houses to exploit the demand for Barbadian goods. They would provide the export services for Barbadians who do not want to bother or do not have the means to export themselves.

More trade missions could be encouraged on a regular basis to visit Barbados, primarily with the aim of buying Barbadian goods. This has application especially to the fashion industry where the manufacturers can come together and sell their products in a co-operative venture and not compete against each other.

Piggy-backing is another option where a manufacturer already trading overseas arranges to sell other products with his own, for example, solar water heaters with furniture. These arrangements would have to be agreed on: fees, terms for the facility, and so on, and the spirit is one of co-operation.

The benefits to be gained are several in that there will be no problems of translation. The transactions would be according to Barbadian laws. The revenue paid would be paid through the bank accounts of the individual manufacture. No complex export documentation would be needed. No risks of non-payment due to foreign government intervention. There is no need to arrange overseas shipment.

Indirect exporting in this manner is almost free of the hassles, the only trade-off is that profit margins may be less than direct marketing, but the pros far outweigh the cons.

Need to Preserve Our Barbadian Culture

Despite myriad definitions, culture is in essence the total way of life of a people.

There is a great interest in the resurgence of culture of the majority of Bajans, especially these of African descent, but it is not an easy task after the cultural emasculation done on the majority of our people by our colonial masters and the acculturation done by American television programmes and lifestyles.

Do we as Bajans have the will to pass on our culture to future generations through socialisation. Our dress, foods, way of life of the young generation do not indicate this at the moment. Technology has influenced our culture. We need only to see the changing role of women and men in our society, with house husbands and working women in the progression towards equality of the sexes.

If we want to preserve the more positive aspects of the remnants of our culture, we must pass them on to our young generation. The types of food which we cooked thirty years ago are not popular today. The way we built our houses, our social environment in the villages, the caring, sharing, the extended family have been downplayed.

It is heartening to see Barbadians of African descent decked in their flowing robes and head gear. It gives distinction to them and to some extent is a challenge to the western mode of dress. Our dances also have relevance although these can vary from occasion to occasion and not have a preponderance of wukking-up. Young Nubians danced before the Pharaohs in Egypt.

The preservation of culture makes a people. Every people's culture shares certain common features although the expression of it differs; the role is the same. It is the way of worshiping God and providing for our needs.

Preserving Bajan Culture

Despite a myriad of definitions culture is in essence our total way of life. There is great interest in the preservation of the culture of Barbadians especially of African descent, but it is not easy after the emasculation done by the colonial masters and after the acculturation done by the media and the lifestyles which we are quick to adopt.

Culture although usually representing the material aspects of life, has other facets. The classification is not only the classical definition of aesthetics and artistic pursuits but includes our beliefs and values, customs, folkways. Barbadian culture embraces our rum shops, our going to church, the way we greet each other with the old clichés, our conventions like shaking hands and aspects of our etiquette. These aspects are hard to change. Our mores such as monogamy, common law relations, the way in which we build our houses, bungalows and the chattel houses, and the way we build our boats are components of our culture. Our rituals and marriage ceremonies, pitching marbles, marble cricket, our food and sports are all components of Barbadian culture.

Ritualistic behaviours can be seen in the way in which our women dress or do their makeup, how men wear their hair and the fashions which they adopt. Barbadian dialect and its pronunciation are part of our culture. Although English is an official language, Bajan sayings, intonations and phraseology are peculiar to us in many cases having African and indigenous roots.

Do we have a wide enough section of young Barbadians to embrace and perpetuate our Bajan culture? Are these capable of passing on our culture to future generations through the process if socialisation? By the lifestyles, dress and the way of life of the young, this seems a difficult undertaking. Technology has influenced our culture and many are acculturated by foreign cultures, mainly the USA.

We must fine tune and preserve the positive aspects of our culture, our language, the foods we eat, our dance e.g. 'wukking up' not the debased form of erotic frenzy, celebrated a few days of the year. We as primarily a black nation, should be sensitized to our origins. We must learn about Africa, its history, culture, geography and ethnic groups and not feel in any way inferior to other races or nationalities.

The preservation of our culture is what will make us a people. Every society has a culture which gives it distinction. This culture is a way and form of worshipping God and it serves the same function in all societies, be they in the Amazon Jungle or the Middle East.

Older Barbadians must sensitise their children to our culture, and it must be shared by a significant proportion of our society. Cultural diversity is a reality, but there are certain factors which at the end of the day are ideally Bajan – the Landship is the best example. Our culture of essence has to be cumulative i.e. handed down (from generations) to each new generation, and there is a role to be played at Primary and

Secondary level schools. It should be dynamic in that it must be adaptive and evolutionary to fulfill the needs of society, despite exposure and bombardments from other cultures. In the New World order Barbadians will have to make their cultural mark on the tabula rasa of civilization.

Racism in Barbados

The definition is that each race has certain qualities or abilities, giving rise to the belief that some races are better than others hence stereotyping and discrimination and hostility towards others. It is a learnt belief because we see that at tender age children of different races study and play together. By observing their parents, and being taught and socialized, young whites develop the qualities of discrimination. By the time they leave school the feature is most marked.

In Barbados there is no racial harmony, but no one rocks the boat. It is more a case of peaceful segregation. We don't live in the same neighbourhoods, whites stick to themselves and mixed marriages between Barbadian blacks and whites are few. To do this would lead to ostracism by their race. Blacks have wealth collectively, but are not aware of the economic clout which they possess. They have gained political power, but the commanding heights of the economy are still possessed by whites, Indians and foreigners.

Democratisation of education offered them some upward social mobility in 60s and 70s and to some extent empowered them, but this is not as marked today. Today, Blacks gained access to older secondary schools en masse and obtained jobs in financial institutions, and corporate entities and more professions.

But, the reality is that today, Blacks still have restricted access to certain clubs, beaches and certain social and economic groupings. Blacks in Barbados have remained passive, which is a legacy of slavery, in which there was no excess land on which many could establish free communities. They were broken psychologically by the plantation regime - hence subjugated to the plantation mentality of selling one's labour and enriching others.

We have tended to deal with the matter superficially and tried to equate it to class which has blinded us to the reality of racism, which is more active, whereas classism as the feelings of superiority and inferiority are acted out daily. Class prejudice is more subtly acted out, although we hear of some incidents. Women in Bim do not marry men out of their class, which in most cases is socially defined by occupation. Some whites treat their pets better than they treat most blacks and we are badmouthed and stereotyped in many instances .The work situation is the same, blacks and whites work together, but go home to their separate domiciles-akin to slavery. Do they ever invite blacks to their homes, although they do the same jobs?

Over the years several black businessmen have been discriminated against by banking policies. The immediate post independence years witnessed an exodus of white Barbadians to New Zealand and Australia. They feared the consequences of blacks 'Taking over". Even the descendants of the indentured servants are prejudiced against blacks. Indian-black marriages are almost unheard of. You can befriend them, but don't marry them!

There are several Bajans of repute whose great grandparents were jet black, yet today they are ashamed of their lineage and don't like to associate with blacks. The system is such that you go to school with them, but on leaving school there is no further interaction except on the job. Segregation is again raising its ugly head at many schools. We stand to see white gated areas in which blacks will be excluded. The whole concept is a pigment of the imagination. It oppresses its victims from attaining their true potential and blights its perpetrators. The problem has to be addressed, not only in Barbados, but globally and a healing arrived at. It among other things hampers the development of the nation, especially its consciousness.' Young generations of white Barbadians will not be guilty of the atrocities of their ancestors unless they continue their old practices'

We can pretend that there is racial harmony, but it is class which draws blacks and whites together on the job, in the fraternities, but the practice of racism is a barrier to unity and hence world progress and peace. It has affected the social and economic structure in all countries in which it is a feature with feelings of superiority, distrust, control and the ability to exploit those deemed inferior.

Need to Clean Up Public Transport System

Now that there will be no increase in bus fares, it is necessary that measures be implemented to alleviate a dismal public transport system, which is costing the country thousands of lost man hours and productivity, through no fault of the workers.

A holistic approach to this service, with both the minibus and the transport board, working towards a synergy which will benefit commuters.

The minibuses need to be regulated. These vehicles provide an invaluable service but the behaviour exhibited by some workers and the general minibus culture, at times leaves a lot to be desired.

Cellphones should be barred because some bus drivers can be seen with these gadgets fastened to their ears. Many transport board buses are over loaded but only the minibuses are offloaded. Where is the equality of treatment? The law enforcement officers are trying their best, but there should be one law for both the Medes and the Persians.

The main competitive advantage which the minibuses possess is reliability and regularity of service. It is still possible for commuters, whose only means of transport is the government owned busses, to be stranded for hours. On occasions one does not see a bus to Howell's and the Ivy and at night to Sargeant Street.

Commuters demand by right, a better service from transport providers. Regularity, flexible hours, reliability, safety and commuter friendly workers are part of the formula.

Some suggestions to the Barbados Transport Board:

- Create a new comprehensive maintenance programme.

- Have adequate rolling stock on the road, especially to service longer routes at peak hours.

- Provide more reliable services.

- Have more commuter friendly drivers.

- End the mash-up and buy-back syndrome.

- Have more flexible timing of busses

- Try to get more mileage out of busses and obviate the need for tax payers money to prop-up the ailing service.

- Improving routing and trafficking of busses. More on-the-spot management and supervision.

- Try to regain some of the minibus market share, through innovative marketing.

- Rationalise the whole operation of the service.

- Downsize the Transport Board to stop placing money in a financial furnace.

- Remove free bus service to school children. Some sort of token fee should be paid.

- Implement a comprehensive transport system.

Many Reasons For Quality Problems

There are myriad reasons for service quality problems in Barbados. Services are mainly dispensed in the presence of customers and hence with the human factor problems are bound to arise. Many service providers exhibit poor presentation skills, conduct themselves inappropriately, and dress improperly.

Front end employees are the sharp end of the service delivery and they need support from the back end of the organization. They need the equipment, such as tools, materials and uniforms to perform their jobs efficiently and effectively. Skills training is essential and so is current information, especially when a new service launces operating procedures.

Failure to deliver

A communication gap occurs in many service operations when there is failure to deliver on promises made, failure to keep customers involved, as well as communicate with them in a manner that they can understand. Some service providers fail to listen to their customers.

In many services there are compelling reasons for offering standardized service to customers. Most customers would welcome being treated in such a manner i.e. like a king, and have their individual needs met and not like mere statistics.

Many organizations in Barbados, some utilities and other profit-driven enterprises, have a short run view of their business when it comes to performance evaluation.

Their yearly financial targets which have to be met, lead to an obsession with cost reductions through increased productivity, to meet their profit targets and stakeholders interests , which is detrimental to building long-run quality service dispensation.

Quality products, quality service leads to long-term customer loyalty.

Bringing Price Controls Not an Easy Task

The price of branded products in Barbados cannot be controlled by price control legislation.

Price is a measure of quality, and there are many determining factors and ways used in arriving at what the customer pays for a product or service, which- in a country that imports such a large percentage of consumer goods – would make such measuring difficult.

Price controls would call for policing enforcing and ensuring compliance. In the end it would be costly, both in terms of time and money, and could have the effect of killing small retailers.

Branded products tend to cost more, in that they contain attributes which are built into the brand. But in the end, we must ask "what is the difference between a leading brand and a lesser brand?"

The targeting of the brand at the market segment which is aimed at the advertising cost, packaging, and other variables account for the higher prices of these goods.

Retailers tend to sell some items at cost such as "loss leaders" in an effort to clear stock or to generate sales of other products.

The entire product range cannot be sold at cost, any reduction in revenue has to be made up on other products. One hardly sees a "branded" product being a "loss leader".

The budget stores which operate in Barbados are doing a good job, with their low frills, high volume, lower-priced product. They specialize in lower margins and high volume sales, but they must still cover their cost with some degree of profit. Customers can see significant savings at some of these outlets.

The larger supermarkets, on the other hand, have good ambiance, "service", and wider product ranges, but incur overheads in terms of staff numbers, displays, advertising, and so on. They are patronized mainly by a specific segment of the market with higher income, taste for expensive goods and services, and less time to shop around.

We do not possess a large enough market for us to develop multiples, which can market their own labels and allow certain goods to be sold at lower prices, than the branded goods and which can help in maintaining "customer loyalty".

The main pricing strategy tends to be full cost pricing in which increments are added for the products and then some sort of margin, before reaching the final cost.

Cellphonemania

The proliferation of cell phones in Barbados, upwards to 300 000 in current use is by no means an accident. We have developed a liking for this gadget and through skilful marketing by the service providers market penetration will continue. From the heavy, cumbersome looking ,first generation of phones, we have moved to the sleek, colourful, versatile ,needless to say expensive instruments, with their several features, which are attracting both the young and old segments of the market alike and the trend will continue.

The product ranges of these phones are wide, from the basic ones, which cost a few dollars to the top of the range, which can cost over $1000.00. The core product of a cell phone is the basic communication gadget with limited features of storing names, phone numbers, texting and other basic features which is what most users, especially the old consumers demand. The core benefits do not change that quickly but the aim of the service provider is to supply the demands of the total market and its needs by identifying, anticipating and satisfying these needs, albeit profitably.

The formal product is what is provided at specified times at specified prices, be it at Easter, Christmas or the New Year; hence the specials and promotions. There is little to choose between competitors, with formal product offers, hence we see service providers marketing similar formal products. Price of the formal product may become the principal reason for customer choice, although slight design and aesthetics of cellphones may be of some importance in customer choice.

The augmented product is both tangible and intangible. Hence the service providers vie for competitive advantage which gives them the edge and consequently can lead to increased market share and profitability. These are the value added, over and above the formal product offer. Hence we see the main producers/brands of cellphones differentiating their products from those of their competitors. The different features cameras, ring tones, sleek and colourful designs, attractive cases and the 'cutting edge' features in design and technology. The image of the brand or the position that it occupies in the customers eyes is always part of the augmented product.

The cell phone providers know this fact very well and their regular advertisements and special offers are attracting more and more owners. Little children feel left out, alienated, when they don't possess a cellphone, their peers avoid them. Some adults may have three even four. It is a frenzy, never before was the need to talk greater. Children carry them to bed; we use them to call friends and loved ones. They can be heard in houses of worship and proliferate the workplace. The conversations are mundane and instances of cheating in examinations, arrangements for rendezvous for crime and violence, small businessmen from the informal economy also use them in their trade. Boys on the block and pimps are in possession of this tool.

We are a nation of consumers and the numbers will grow and as the technology is improved and more mass production is done.   Despite the experts pronouncements of potential harm from the use of these devices it is yet to be seen how customers adjust to this modern miracle of communication.

Part 4 - Foreign Affairs

Black People Just Want Justice

Slavery in every form is a barbaric act and African slavery was among the most atrocious committed against any race. No sound argument can be found to legitimize slavery.

Not only were people of African descent culturally emasculated, but additionally they lost their religion, whole social structure, their agricultural land, their human rights and their equal status.

Land in Africa was common property and with the coming of the Europeans the best land was confiscated and the marginal land left to the indigenous people. Hence, the demise of African agriculture. People of African descent in the Caribbean, have never found the social cohesion since being uprooted from the motherland, hence the semblance of unity which exists today.

The Jews received US $4 billion for the atrocities of Hitler. People of African descent received nothing. Some experts estimate that 20 million blacks were uprooted. Some estimate as many as 100 million. People of African descent don't want to physically go back to Africa, but we must be aware of our origins and be proud of our past.

Every year millions of Americans and Canadians of European descent trek to Europe to the birth places of their ancestors and relatives. We as black people don't like to associate with things African, even many of our university graduates who should know better.

Racism is ridiculous. It is endemic in every society and in almost all cases people of African descent are at the lowest echelon of society.

There will be no peace until justice and fair play and racism are obliterated from the face of this earth. People of African descent are loving, long-offering and forgiving. South Africa now has a black government and we have not seen revenge for the wicked treatment at the hands of oppressors under the apartheid system.

We criticize Robert Mugabe president of Zimbabwe and call for sanctions. But, what about Cecil Rhodes et al who appropriated these lands from Blacks. Was this justice? When Rhodes and other colonisers were on the rampage, Britain was silent and gave legality to these actions.

Uninformed people ought to read Eric Williams' **Capitalism And Slavery**, Walter Rodney's **How Europe Underdeveloped Africa** as well as many other texts on Africa. The western press constantly by its sheer strength can distort our views.

Africa's Wealth Being Exploited Again

Africa is being colonized and subjected to another spate of economic exploitation, this time around by the Chinese. With its vast deposits of minerals and oil, once again the mother country's wealth is up for exploitation by the world's newest emergent superpower.

China has signed agreements with Nigeria, Zaire and other mineral rich countries for the exploitation of these essential and strategic minerals, to fuel in vast industries and what most likely will result in cheap labour, exploitation and the flooding of African markets with cheap goods all without the development of African countries.

These agreements are with African leaders who enrich themselves while the vast masses of Africans are among the poorest people in the world. Many rural citizens of Africa have never had access to electricity, potable water, balanced nutrition, modern health care, education, or housing.

The lip service paid to their cause by the leaders of the world's richest countries, who were the ones responsible for the rape of Africa - the British, French, Belgians, Portuguese, Spaniards, even Italy and Germany – had their hands in the under-development of this vast and rich continent.

The transatlantic slave trade is analogous to what oil is in this era.

Slave trade business was big business and its magnitude was perhaps even greater than that of oil in this civilization. It has been estimated that to quantify the value of the transatlantic slave trade would run into the trillions of US dollars.

This is the equivalent to the annual GDPs of some of the richer countries in today's setting.

Monetary reparation is the main issue at hand. Acceptance, remorse and the official pardon for having committed this heinous and barbaric act against a whole race would start the process; followed by assistance in the form of relevant technological transfers, opening up the markets for the produce of African states and their descendants, facilitating exports and rebates on imports from the rich countries.

The offering of scholarships free of cost in developmental fields to students of African countries and their descendants in the Diaspora and the realization of their equality.

Equality of treatment for the same people. A realization of the equal sovereignty of people of the diaspora; a say at Group of eight deliberations and the United Nations, especially in the field of economics, social development, and environmental issues; and a status on the World Trade Organization meetings and the International Monetary Fund.

Is this too much to ask?

Powerbase

The traditional interpretation of power, as advantage enjoyed by persons or groups, needs to be re defined if integration of the peoples of the world is to be accelerated. Power has been seen as a tool to be used by people against others. This has become part of the culture of division and conflict, which has existed throughout the past several centuries.

Power has in general been attributed to individuals, factions, peoples, races, classes and nations. It has been associated with men, rather than women and has endowed and conferred on its beneficiaries the ability to acquire usually, material things, to suppress, to dominate others, to resist, win and even conquer.

These factors have been responsible for setbacks in the amelioration of the condition of the human family and have hampered advances in civilization. But today, when problems are global in nature, be they environmental, economic, the threat of war, famine, or the quest for equality, by races and sexes, this concept of power, has lost most of its effectiveness. In essence it is of no utility to social and economic development.

Those who still adhere to the old notion of power find their schemes becoming more and more frustrating. The old notion of power is useless to the needs of future generations. It is like applying modern surgical procedures to automotive technology. With advancing civilization, the understanding of power and how it is used has to be freed from this limited concept. Yet, over the centuries, and despite these limits, men and women, of varying backgrounds, have harnessed a range of resources within themselves.

The power of truth, as an agent of change has been associated with some of the greatest advances in philosophy, religion, arts and sciences, which have resulted in mobilizing human responses as does the influences of individual human beings or human societies. How much greater will be the influence of unity?

The consciousness of humanity will only be elicited when institutions in society, which exercise power and authority, are governed by principles that are in coherence with the influence of those who are subjected to their power. The power brokers need to win the confidence, respect and genuine support of those whom they seek to govern. They need to consult openly with all those whose interests are affected by their decisions, to assess as objectively as possible, the real needs and aspirations of the communities they serve, to benefit from scientific and moral advancement in order to maximize the utility of the communities resources, including the energies of its members. Maintaining unity among the members of society and the administrative institutions is of primal importance. There must be a search for justice in all matters.

Such principles can only operate in a truly democratic culture. Not a democracy that despite making impressive contributions to human progress in the past endorses partisanship and is today sullied by cynicism, apathy and corruption. As people become more educated, nominations, electioneering and solicitation are being rendered more and more unattractive and are in need of refinement, if the interests of society are to be met collectively.

The power moguls need to see things globally, not only at a local or national level. They must hold themselves responsible for the welfare of humanity.

Tyrant Gone, But No Peace for Iraq

America has removed the tyrant Saddam Hussein, but essentially there are tyrants in the so-called democracies and in other societies. America has made it worse for Iraq.

The initial reasons for the invasion – arms of mass destruction and the removal of the tyrant – have been dispelled.

United states President George Bush was after the world's third- largest tract of oil reserves and he has obtained it at the expense of thousands of innocent Iraqi lives and the destruction of the country's infrastructure and economy. The situation in Iraq is one of anarchy and violence.

We are aware of Bush's and US Vice–President Dick Cheney's vested oil interests. The estimate is that the US uses about one billion tons of this precious commodity annually. Oil is the lifeblood of modern society and the US and the developed countries need it to support their way of life.

America now proposes a democratic election in Iraq, but this would be a very difficult task with the current anarchy and bloodshed in this country, where the only jobs available are in the military and the police force.

America does not care about the Iraqi people as much as they do about the man on the moon. They've got the oil and now it's time to move on to Iran and North Korea.

With Bush's re-election and the continuance of his fight against terrorists, this world will continue to be a very dangerous place.

Islam, like Christianity, has many sects, and many of these are incensed by the actions of the US.

Peace can only come when justice and equity are at the core of our activities.

Oil Prices Rises

The world is feeling the effects of high crude oil prices. The supply of oil, the life blood of modern society, spare capacity is as low as 2%. OPEC, the oil exporting cartel has not improved capacity significantly within the last five years. To some extent it has been caught short, essentially the whole world has been caught short recently.

The situation has been precipitated by the burgeoning demand for this black gold. The continuous high demand in the developed world and the burgeoning economies of Communist China with the same greed as the capitalists and a population of over 1.3 billion souls and India with its 1 billion plus. This economic growth has set off a spiral of demand for oil and its byproducts and all that go with the trappings of a materialistic civilization and it will only increase with time.

The rush to drill for oil in amounts and conditions which would have been deemed uneconomic, and the speed with which the deposits in Nigeria, Gabon, the Cameroons and the South Sudan in Africa are all being exploited although the citizens in these countries only consume a decimal of the oil consumed and are amongst some of the world's poorest. The paradox exist in Nigeria where despite being a leading producer, gasoline and cooking oil are rationed and hundreds have lost their lives trying to siphon off these commodities from pipelines.

The Secretary General of OPEC has iterated that oil production has not peaked. There are estimations that of oil potential 1/3 has been used, 1/3 is in reserves and 1/3 is yet to be discovered. The vast reserves of heavy crude in Venezuela and the Athabasca Tar sands of Alberta, Canada are alternative sources yet to be tapped. It pays to keep oil prices high, market demand continues to grow, oil in the modern world is essential as a fuel and as a raw material for petrochemicals and plastics.

With high demand existing there is no great rush to research other forms of energy like wind and wave energy although European, American and some developing countries are initiating this effort.

One does not know if and when oil depletion will occur but the Saudi oil Minister whose country possesses by far the greatest proven reserves has indicated that around 2080 a crisis situation may occur where reserves may be as low as 10%. Within the next 30-40 years demand and supply should continue to rest with the oil lobby trying feverishly to keep the price as high as possible. The price in New York and London, the premier commodity markets, has risen to over US$100 recently and there are predictions that it can go as high as US$120 if the current trend continues.

Other factors which have contributed to this crisis have been the increasing demand resulting from the proliferation of motor cars and larger vehicles in spite of stagnant gasoline production. Alternative technologies like wind, hydrogen, solar power have been slowly adapted in the market place. The destabilisation of The Middle East is the chief source of oil production, by the US 'war on terrorism'. The modern world's economy is built on oil, this is so because of its efficiency as and energy source, modern transportation the petrochemical industry plastics and lubricants.

The proliferation of larger vehicles mainly SUVs, which despite the fact that car manufacturers are more efficient with new models, this SUV segment with more powerful engines and consumption increases demand for gasoline. The affluence of modern societies, if we should take the possession of motor cars as an indicator of wealth has increased the demand for oil.

The price of oil is not determined by demand and supply but moreso by speculation in commodity futures. Political, economic, environmental and other factors can set off a panic or frenzy among the gamblers in New York and London for which the whole world, especially The Third World pays and the only true beneficiaries are the multinational companies.

OPEC, the Organisation Of Petroleum Exporting Countries cartel, is not a price setter but a quota allocator among its members. Prices are set in the stock markets of New York and London. There is need for alternatives to oil in the future, but the transition to an era where oil as a fuel and a source of energy is not as dominant, is a long way off, given the yet bountiful reserves of oil.

The high cost of research and development of new sources of energy which although available, are not yet seen as urgent in that the same companies which control oil exploration, production refining and distribution are in the forefront of alternative energy development and possess the resources to develop these resources. There is no immediate rush to develop alternatives in the face of billion dollar profits which are being made in the current market situation. A lower oil price could only dampen the furtherance of research into new sources of energy, although this is desirable.

In the interim the cost of petroleum products will rise, transport cost, most manufactured goods, especially those which use oil as a raw material plastic, synthetics, agricultural produce, electricity and other energy sources in short an exhaustive list of products and services. The burden will not only fall on businesses but families especially those with low incomes. Globally, countries in general which have no indigenous oil reserves and have to import the modern 'life blood', of this civilization will continue to be hardest hit and many will experience economic tailspins.

The main beneficiaries of oil price rises, now hovering around $100.00 per barrel, will be the multi-national giants which control the oil industry from exploration to distribution to the final consumer. The billion dollar profits to ExxonMobil, Shell, BP, Texaco, Total, Chevron et al will be the bottom line of the rises in price of this essential product.

Blacks, be Proud of our Origins

As an attendee to the opening ceremony of the Conference on Racism, I have a few comments to make. I am not a racist, but permit me to err on the side of justice and fair play.

I was elated by the dress of the audience and the spirit which existed among those of us who are conscious of the plight of African descendants globally.

The only people who are going to tackle and surmount the myriad problems of discrimination, abject poverty of African people, disease stereotyping of their people, are people of African descent themselves.

The message that came across from the statements made by the speakers was that they were gathered for serious discussion and deliberation. The process of racial healing needs to go beyond Durban. Strategies need to be devised to level the field for people of African descent.

The mere reality is that AIDS (700 new infections in Mozambique daily), poverty, and exploitation affects Blacks globally. We are the hungriest, sickliest race in the world and our condition was precipitated by European expansionism in Africa. We can sit in Barbados and pretend that we have levelled the playing field and that we are accepted by Whites.

But try what you may, we are never accepted.

Let me state that there are many genuine people of non-African descent. In my travail and travels I've met some, but not many. As a pupil of Lodge School in the 1960's and 1970's, I saw and experienced racial discrimination and it has left me with an indelible opposition to the process.

Many black Barbadians indulge in self-denial. They hate things Africa. This land, 95 percent populated by people of African stock, practices self-hatred and scorns those of us who have the gumption to wear their traditional dress or promote things African. Don't Americans and people of European stock flock back to the homes of their ancestors in Britain, Germany or wherever?

People of European descent are proud of their Irish, Polish, British and German ancestry and continue their cultural rites and ceremonies. They are proud and do not hide their past origins by living in self-denial.

I questioned the presence of non-Whites at the conference opening. Why? Because I thought the whole spirit was one of seriousness and carrying forward the black cause. Are Africans invited to the conferences of the G8, that is, the First World countries (United States, Germany, Britain, France, Canada, Japan and/or Russia or Italy)? The answer is no, and these countries control the world – economically, politically, socially and culturally, and forcefully promote their global vested interest.

No umbrella body in this world is going to pursue the plight of African people globally. Barbados has the opportunity to be the venue where future decisions could be made to enhance the people of African descent and our progeny in the future. This is serious business.

With AIDS threatening our people both in Africa and the Caribbean, with the abject poverty and deprivation even in our neighboring Caribbean islands, we need to seriously sit and deliberate on our future.

Economic power is not going to gain us acceptance. This will come when we come together, accept our origins and pursue our agenda. In this new, evolving world order, what will distinguish the peoples of the world will be their culture.

I fail to see adopting Western ways as advancing the cause of African descendants. We can pretend, but this will not suffice our consciences and deep feeling. We must carry on for the road is long, the journey tedious and painstaking.

Third World Debt Trap

The Developing Countries and the Third World are being placed in a position from which it is becoming increasingly difficult to extricate themselves.

The powerbrokers of this world, such as, the G8 countries have confined us in so many ways it would take volumes to really start to understand this bind in which Third World countries are placed.

The side-effects of this world process have been grinding poverty, lack of infrastructure, high mortality rates, disease and all the maladies which face countries, namely in Africa, the Caribbean, Latin America and parts of Asia.

In many instances the corruption of governments, lack of education and underdevelopment of indigenous resources have all contributed to the backwardness of these countries.

The First World countries and their adjuncts the International Monetary Fund (IMF), the World Bank, the World Trade Organisation and these other institutions have all placed developing, usually non-European countries in a death trap of poverty.

The Asian Tigers, at a juncture in the '90s were on the verge of becoming First World Countries, but circumstances which are still nebulous saw to it that they remained "developing countries" for example, South Korea and Taiwan.

Globalisation in its current form, where the First Word Countries are and will continue to be the main benefactors is anathema. The push for free trade and trade liberalization has opened up the markets in most Third World countries to a deluge of manufactured goods and services from the first world countries whereas the Third World countries still in many cases only trade in primary commodities, the terms of trade, vis a vis manufactured goods, is horrendously skewed in favour of the First World countries.

Third World countries have to compete among one another for markets, with mainly primary products. Barbadian sugar for example competes with that of Brazil, India and other lower cost countries. We are daily becoming more and more the "victims" of this scheme of things.

A recent visit to Britain was a revelation of the ever widening gap and in some cases a clash between the developed and developing countries. A guesstimate will say that the lag of development in many cases was between 20 years and 30 years.

Rural St. Vincent is reminiscent of Barbados in the 60s except for occasional monuments and mementos of prosperity. Barbadians should be eternally thankful for some of the bounties which we have.

A social security system, an educational system which is evolving, a fairly good road network, a health care system which is available to all. The denizens of the United States, the world's richest nation, are not all covered by health insurance. Millions don't have access to health care. Barak Obama is feverishly trying to rectify this anomaly in the 21 century, despite fierce opposition from the tea party segment of the opposition Republican Party.

In Britain, soccer is the religion and beer the opium. We have our beliefs and addictions. Youth, globally are in crisis, and the reasons for this are myriad. It is possible and lawful to use marijuana that is a controlled quantity in Britain. The Netherlands tried a similar experiment and it has had devastating consequences.

There are many Third World countries which have had to depend on illegal drugs for their economic survival. The drug lords and the pushers have had a field day.

The demise of the banana industry in St. Vincent and the Windwards, precipitated by the action of the United States in protecting Chiquita and Dole, has been the primary reason for the collapse of the banana industry in the Windwards. Hence the switch to another "cash crop". Also our rum, even Mount Gay, the first and arguably one of the best in the world is being challenged by US preferential treatment of inferior brands.

The whole question of aid to developing countries is another complex problem. It is estimated that for every dollar the United States gives in aid, it makes $1.50, usually as a result of recipient countries having to buy American-manufactured goods and or technology, as the case may be as a condition for granting this aid.

The whole indebtedness of the Third World countries means that many are in a debt trap, a continuous cycle of mendicancy from which they are unable to break free. Mighty Brazil in one year paid US$1 billion in interest to the lending agencies.

As a developing country Barbados is no longer in the hands of the IMF and this condition is expected to continue. When one enters the clutches of this body, one's currency never regains its parity, the result of inevitable devaluations. Governments have to cut back on social services, for example, health. Privatisation is the norm as many governments have to divest their interest in many public institutions which a in many cases are of benefit to the masses of the poor and underprivileged within their midst. Transport costs rise, prices rise and a whole chain of events occur which leave the citizens, especially the poor, in a state of ever decreasing quality of life. This situation is compounded when the country has no indigenous food supply or industrial base.

Political leaders of Third World countries of necessity have to be strong, visionary and committed to the fight, if those whom they govern are to maintain a respectable standard of living and not be mere hewers of wood and drawers of water.

About The Author

Philip Hunte was born on 4th December 1955 and was raised in Ashbury, which is a sugar plantation in St. George, Barbados. He attended St. Jude's Primary School (1960-1966), The Lodge School (1966-1973), and The Barbados Community College (1973-1975). He has worked as a civil-servant from 1976 to present while completing external studies with the Chartered Institute of Marketing, and Birmingham City University, UK.

"Change is the only constant." Heraclitus

www.ingramcontent.com/pod-product-compliance
Lightning Source LLC
Chambersburg PA
CBHW070747290526
45795CB00002B/508